LANERCOS

CUMI

Graham D. Keevill

LANERCOST CROSS BASE *page 15*
The shaft is now inside the church, in the north aisle's blocked door

CHURCHYARD *page 16*

EAST END OF CHURCH *page 4*
Built in the 12th and 13th centuries; the ruined choir and transepts still stand to almost their full height

CHAPTER HOUSE *page 8*
Where the canons met daily to discuss business

Visitors to Lanercost Priory today are likely to be attracted here by the tangible sense of peace, tranquillity and worship, and by the beauty of its setting. These are certainly important qualities, but they hide an often turbulent past. A place of worship since the twelfth century, Lanercost's setting close to the Scottish border meant that the priory was always vulnerable to attack during the Anglo-Scottish wars of the fourteenth century, and in 1311 Robert Bruce himself raided it. Edward I and his retinue stayed here for more than five months in 1306–7 on their way north, putting a severe strain on the priory's resources.

After the priory's dissolution under Henry VIII Lanercost passed to the Dacre family, who converted part of it – notably the Dacre Hall – into a comfortable residence. Part of the nave of the priory church continued in use as a parish church: it was reroofed and sympathetically restored in the nineteenth century, and is still in use today. In contrast, the ruined choir and transepts, which stand almost to their full height, form a dramatic silhouette. This guidebook contains a tour of the extensive priory remains, the parish church, the Dacre Hall and the rest of the precinct, and traces Lanercost's eventful history from medieval times to the present day.

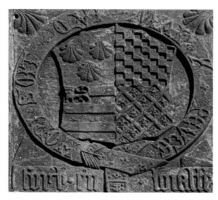

*Above: The coat of arms of the Dacre family on
the west front of Lanercost Priory proclaims
their patronage of the monastery. The Dacres
assumed control over Lanercost in 1315, but
patronage passed to a different line of the family
in 1542 in the aftermath of Henry VIII's
Dissolution of the Monasteries (see page 25). The
scallop shells (top left) were the Dacres' emblem,
while the chequerboard (top right) was that of the
de Vaux family, the priory's first patrons*

*Lanercost Priory
Brampton, Cumbria CA8 2HQ
Tel. 01697 73030
Visit our website at www.english-heritage.org.uk*

*Published by English Heritage
1 Waterhouse Square, 138-142 Holborn,
London EC1N 2ST
© English Heritage 2003
First published by English Heritage 2003
Reprinted 2006, 2008, 2010, 2012, 2015
Revised reprint 2014
Photographs © English Heritage, unless otherwise stated*

*Editor: Katy Carter. Design: Pauline Hull.
Plan: Richard Morris. Picture research: Diana Phillips.
Photography: Bob Skingle.*

*Printed in England by Park Communications Ltd.
ISBN 978 1 85074 847 2
C20, 06/15, 04163*

❖ CONTENTS ❖

3	TOUR OF THE PRIORY
3	THE RUINS
3	*The Cloister*
4	*East End of Priory Church*
7	*East Cloister Range*
8	*South Cloister Range*
10	*Dacre Tower*
10	*Laver*
10	*West Cloister Range*
11	DACRE HALL
12	THE PARISH CHURCH
15	THE PRECINCT
15	*Vicarage and Vicar's Pele*
16	*Churchyard*
16	*Abbey Farm*
17	*Outer Gatehouse and Precinct Wall*
18	HISTORY OF THE PRIORY
18	FOUNDATION
19	THE AUGUSTINIANS
20	MEDIEVAL PATRONS
20	LIFE AT THE PRIORY
22	EDWARD I AND LANERCOST
24	DEBTS AND DECLINE
25	THE DISSOLUTION OF THE MONASTERIES
26	LANERCOST AND THE DACRES
28	THE 18th AND 19th CENTURIES
31	ARTS AND CRAFTS AT LANERCOST
31	LATER HISTORY
	FEATURES
6	The Tombs
9	Roman Stonework and Altars
14	The Lanercost Cross
21	Daily Life at Lanercost
32	FURTHER READING
Inside back cover	PLAN OF THE PRIORY

TOUR OF THE PRIORY

Lanercost Priory is an unusual historic site because there are several distinct areas to visit, each fascinating in its own right. The main elements (church, ruins, Dacre Hall and precinct) are now in separate ownership and management, but each started life within one unified establishment – the priory. The break-up of the monastic estate after the Dissolution is reflected in the lack of a single, obvious route around the site. Indeed there are many ways to go around Lanercost, and this is part of its charm. The following guided tour largely follows the route of the existing English Heritage audiotour around the ruins, before moving on to the church and then the monastic precinct. *If the priory ruins are closed, begin your tour on page 11.*

THE RUINS
The Cloister
Enter the ruins through the English Heritage ticket office (in the slype, *or passageway). You are now in the medieval cloister.*

The cloister was a simple square courtyard attached to the south side of the priory church, with the canons' domestic buildings around

Below: The church and cloister, seen from the south. This view clearly shows the square layout of the medieval cloister, with a garth (garden) in the middle – used as the vicarage vegetable garden in Victorian times

ENGLISH HERITAGE/SKYSCAN BALLOON PHOTOGRAPHY

Right: The south wall of the church. The slight changes in colour and pattern of the stones on the wall face show how it was built in stages. The corbels – stones projecting from the wall face – supported the roof over the cloister walkway

Below: The door to the south transept is very plain. It is flanked by a small round-headed niche to the north (left), and a cupboard to the south, probably used for storing books. You can also see further corbels here

the other three sides. Access to this area was largely restricted to the prior and canons: it served as the place set aside for private reading and meditation, and it also gave them constant access to the church. You can see two blocked doors in the south wall of the nave, and an open one through to the crossing and choir in the west wall of the south transept. The western nave door is quite plain, but the eastern one is much more elaborate, showing that it was the more important.

The south wall of the church was one of the first parts of the priory to be built. Look at the walls around the cloister and you will also see plenty of evidence for the lean-to roofs that went all round it, giving the canons a continuous covered corridor to walk round. Look for the horizontal scars where the roofs joined the walls, and

the corbels that supported the timber framing under the roof. You may notice different scar and corbel heights in places, showing that the roof level changed at one time.

East End of Priory Church

Go through the door in the west wall of the south transept and walk to the centre of the crossing, beneath the tower, where the canons sat in their choir stalls during services. Face east towards the ruins with the parish church at your back.

Standing here can give you a curiously 'inside out' impression of the medieval church. The wall behind you with three tall, pointed windows that provide an intriguing glimpse into the parish church is little more than 250 years old. It filled in the great open arch that once gave access from the nave to the crossing where you are now standing. There would have been a timber screen (rood) further back in the nave, and the parish congregation could only catch glimpses of services being celebrated in the area beyond the crossing.

The presbytery lay straight ahead of you, with the high altar against its end wall. This is where the main masses were celebrated. The chambers to either side of you, the transepts, contained secondary but important chapels. One of these was used for a chantry set up in 1503 by Mabel Dacre (see page 26); this probably lay

lancet (pointed) windows and arcades rising straight to the clerestory (the top level of windows), and is essentially two-storey in concept. The north side, by contrast, has more squat arcade piers to allow for an additional middle storey above, the triforium. The slender shafts with carefully moulded tops (capitals) and bases give an elegance that contrasts with the earlier architecture of the south side. The north half and

Left: The early thirteenth-century clerestory windows, seen here in the north transept, allowed daylight to flood into the church. The clerestory passage provided access to the top of the walls around the church. An access door for the passage can be seen in the north-west corner of the north transept

to your left (north), where you can see the fine tomb of Sir Humphrey and Mabel Dacre, probably erected after her death in 1510 (see box, page 6). The south transept – to your right – contains the tomb of their son, Thomas, Lord Dacre, and his wife, Lady Elizabeth. This was put up between 1516 and 1525.

This is the perfect place to appreciate the lofty grandeur of the priory's late twelfth- to early thirteenth-century architecture. At first glance the walls and windows probably look much the same, but look closer and you will see that the north and south halves of the building are quite different. The south side (to your right) has tall

Right: The presbytery and side chapels at the east end of the priory church. Note the contrast between the late twelfth-century tall arches with one set of windows over them on the south side (to the right), and the early thirteenth-century squat arches with two tiers of windows above to the north

THE TOMBS

Lanercost's patrons were buried in the priory's east end from the death of Randolf, the first Lord Dacre, in 1339 to the twentieth century. The ornate tomb of Sir Humphrey Dacre in the north transept was set up after his widow Lady Mabel's death in 1510. Humphrey had a turbulent political career in the mid-fifteenth century but ultimately secured his family's possession of Lanercost before dying in 1485.

The canopied tomb of Lord Thomas and Lady Elizabeth Dacre in the south transept was made about ten years after Sir Humphrey's and is of similar design, but more elaborate. The carved decoration would have been brightly painted, but both tombstones have suffered much erosion. Lord Thomas had an important role in the English victory at Flodden in 1513, and was promoted to be warden of the East, West and Middle marches in 1515. Thomas died on campaign in Scotland on 24 October 1525.

Below: This exquisite terracotta effigy by the renowned sculptor Sir Edgar Boehm (1834–90) commemorates Elizabeth Dacre Howard, daughter of George and Rosalind Howard. She died on 17 July 1883, only four months old

Above: The tomb of Lord Thomas and Lady Elizabeth Dacre, in the south arcade of the presbytery. This tomb, like that of Sir Humphrey, displays the family heraldry with the Dacre scallops and de Vaux chequerboard. (Reconstruction by Peter Dunn)

Above: The tomb of Sir Humphrey Dacre and his wife, Lady Mabel, in the north transept chapel. The tomb originally supported life-size effigies of Humphrey and Lady Mabel. Its heraldry proudly proclaims the Dacre lineage and achievements

Above: The tomb of Charles Howard (1867–1912), tenth Earl of Carlisle, by the Scottish architect Robert Lorimer. The use of the Dacre scallop shells emphasises the continuity of interest through many generations of patronage at Lanercost

the east end of the presbytery are of late twelfth- to early thirteenth-century date, while the south transept and arcade is late twelfth-century in date. This and the south wall of the nave are the earliest parts of the priory, and they prove that the church was planned to be cross-shaped from the start.

Take some time to look at the tombs of the Dacre and Howard families in the east end (see box), before leaving this area through the door in the end wall of the south transept.

East Cloister Range

You are now entering the east cloister range. Walk forward across the foundations of the first room, a vestry where robes, altar cloths and other items would have been stored. Notice that two wall lines have been laid out on your left as you walk away from the transept. Stop inside the second room, and turn back to face the transept.

The buildings on the east side of the cloister were torn down to their foundations in the immediate aftermath of the Dissolution, but the end wall of the south transept contains several clues about how they were arranged. First, you can see where the roof used to be from the diagonal stone projections that meet under the central window towards the top of the wall. Second, look above

Above: The crossing of the priory church looking north from the south transept, with the eighteenth-century east window of the parish church to the left. The priory was easily the tallest building in the area, and the tower over the crossing would have enhanced the visual effect of height. The crenellations (battlements) on top of the tower originally continued all round the church, and perhaps reflected the priory's fourteenth-century troubles

Above: The angle of the roof over the twelfth-century east cloister range is clearly visible on the end wall of the south transept. You can also see the scars of the two side walls of the east range, rebuilt in the mid-thirteenth century

Below: The priory seen from the south-east. The outline of the thirteenth-century chapter house can be seen in the foreground

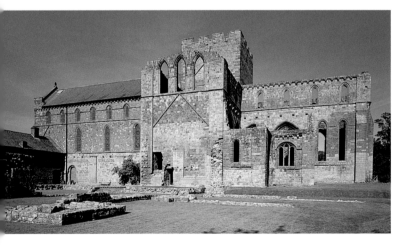

the ground-floor doorway you walked through and you will see another door immediately above it to the left. This marks the entry into the canons' dormitory, which ran along the first floor of the east range. For night-time services, the canons descended the night stairs which led directly from their **dormitory** into the church via this doorway. The holes for the floor joists can be seen to the right of the door.

The east range also contained one of the most important rooms in the priory, the **chapter house**. This room was a common feature of all monasteries. The community would meet here daily to discuss religious matters, to deal with internal discipline and to listen to a chapter of their rule. The original chapter house was a small room contained within the width of the range, but the new one created when this part of the

priory was rebuilt in the thirteenth century was detached from it to the east. The room was much grander and larger than the old one, and its wide foundations suggest that it was taller than before. Like many others, it may have been lavishly decorated in stone and paint.

South Cloister Range

Walk along the east side of the cloister and enter the roofed building on the south side of the cloister, through the door in front of you.

The south side of the cloister was where the canons ate meals together, in a refectory (dining room) on the first floor above this room. The refectory was another victim of the Dissolution. Silence was the rule here as elsewhere in the priory, and the canons used sign language if they needed to communicate. Only one person was allowed to speak – at each meal a canon would read from the Bible or another holy book. Beneath the refectory the ground floor undercroft, in which you are now standing, provided plenty of space for storage of food and drink.

The vaulted undercroft is one of Lanercost's finest features, built like the second chapter house during the mid-thirteenth century. Walk along to the west end, where you will see a fireplace in the south wall. The last three bays were known as the warming room, the only place where the canons were allowed to keep warm in front of a fire. Look carefully and you will see that board games have been scratched into the sills of the window seats in the end (west) wall of the room. Warmth was not the only enjoyment here!

Below: Masons' marks like this one from the undercroft can be seen on many stones around the priory. They were used to show who had been responsible for building the walls

Above: The fine vaulted undercroft of the south cloister range was used for storage of food and drink. The west end contained the warming room where the canons were allowed the comfort of a hearth

ROMAN STONEWORK AND ALTARS

❖ ❖

The walls of the priory include several pieces of Roman inscriptions. The medieval masons chose them simply because they were useful for building, and they often hacked off letters or decoration. You can see one example in the cloister, in the massive chimney of the Dacre Hall in the west range. The opening at its base has part of an inscription above

it, while the fragment of a statue to the right may also be Roman. The undercroft contains replicas of Roman altars and tombstones found near Lanercost over the last 200 years.

A Roman inscription on a stone re-used within the chimney stack of the Dacre Hall. It records building work on Hadrian's Wall by the century of Cassius Priscus of the sixth cohort

Above: The south wall of the undercroft. The refectory lay at first-floor level above the undercroft

Above right: The Dacre Tower became part of the fine house fashioned by Thomas Dacre. The principal rooms were on the top two floors, where there are fine windows. The first floor, where large fireplaces and ovens can be seen internally, was the kitchen, conveniently situated to serve the Dacre Hall

Below: The medieval laver in the north wall of the refectory undercroft, where the monks washed before meals

Dacre Tower

Now retrace your steps and leave the undercroft by one of the doors in the south wall.

The priory kitchen would have stood here, but little of this can be seen now. The tower to your right, however, is another impressive part of the ruins, although its history is uncertain. The building may be medieval in origin, but it was heavily rebuilt by the Dacre family after the Dissolution, when they converted parts of the cloister into a house (see page 27). Enter through the door in front of you, and look up to see the many doors, windows and fireplaces in its four storeys.

Laver

Go back through the west end of the undercroft and re-enter the cloister.

Immediately to your right on the outside wall is the canons' laver (wash basin). The four pointed arches have been destroyed, but the remaining decoration shows how beautiful this feature would have been. The basin itself has also long gone, but the vertical slots for water pipes and drainage can still be seen.

Right: The west range of the cloister. The chimney breast to the left is post-medieval and belongs to the Dacre residence. The first-floor windows are also post-medieval. The roof was lowered during the Dacres' time in residence; the steeper medieval pitch is visible on the south wall of the church

West Cloister Range

The west side of the cloister seems to have provided more storage space for the canons on the ground floor; at the south end was a parlour where they could converse with visitors. There were probably guest rooms or private rooms for the prior on the first floor. The west range became the focal point of the Dacre family's new house after the Dissolution, and most of what you see today belongs to this period. The ground floor is now quite plain (though parts of its vaulted ceiling survive), but the first floor contains one of Lanercost's great glories – the Dacre Hall.

To view Dacre Hall and continue your tour you need to leave English Heritage's property. Walk along the west side of the cloister and leave through the ticket office and shop. Turn left for the entrance to Dacre Hall.

DACRE HALL

This was where the Dacres (see pages 26–7) entertained in style, in a single room stretching nearly the full length of the range (it is now divided by the modern stage). It was well lit from windows in the east and west walls. The grand sixteenth-century fireplace, in what was originally the centre of the east wall, provided warmth. It bears the date 1586 and initials 'CD', of Christopher Dacre, who must have continued the work of his father, Thomas, in creating the hall from the old priory buildings. Three other fireplaces, probably earlier, were at some stage blocked up: two in the west wall, and one in the east. The elaborate oak overmantel now at the north end of the west wall dates from the time of Christopher's son, Henry Dacre. It bears the date 1618, and the coats of arms of his grandfather Thomas (left), his parents (centre), and himself

Right: Dacre Hall today, looking north-west towards the overmantel returned to the hall in 2012 from the Bowes Museum

ELLIE HATT

(right). It may once have adorned the fireplace now blocked behind it, or another in this room or in Dacre Tower.

Traces of wall paintings dating from the creation of the hall in the mid sixteenth-century remain. They are the most important surviving examples of the time in north-west England and the best of them are on the north wall, where columns support an ornate frieze featuring an angel and, immediately below it, the head and wings of a griffin. The small room on the other side of the north wall, known as the scriptorium (not open to the public), also has some good-quality decoration of the Dacre period, consisting of a plaster frieze that features cherubs supporting shields.

ALAN SAWYER

Above: Detail of the oak overmantel dating from 1618 in Dacre Hall, showing the arms of Sir Thomas Dacre (d.1565)

THE PARISH CHURCH

Now walk back towards the church. Stand back to admire the elegance of the west front, Lanercost's finest architectural feature.

The tall pointed windows rest on a blind arcade over the great west door. The gable end still has its medieval statue of the priory's patron saint, Mary Magdalene. The panels to either side display the coats of arms

of Thomas, Lord Dacre to the left (dated between 1518 and 1525) and perhaps the priory itself to the right. High up at the north-west corner of the building are two carved stone heads, traditionally identified as King Edward I and Queen Eleanor.

Now enter the church.

The compromises that had to be made at the Dissolution and afterwards when converting the former monastic church for parish use are still very evident. The ruins of the east end loom through the window built into the crossing arch in the eighteenth

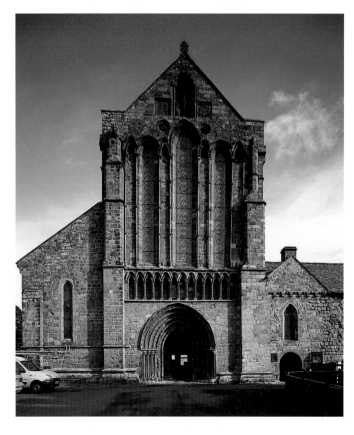

Left: The priory's west front is of exceptional quality. The multiple arches and columns surrounding the door – which, unusually, is slightly off-centre – give way to a continuous row of blind (windowless) arches. The three tall, slender windows emphasise the height of the elevation

Above: The interior of the parish church, looking east. The thirteenth-century aisle with its simple arcade piers contrasts with the tall lancets set at 'first floor' level in the late twelfth-century south wall of the nave, blank except for the two blocked doors into the cloister

century, while the chancel is a late nineteenth-century adaptation of the eastern bay of the priory nave. The single north aisle also ensures that the interior is asymmetrical and irregular. Despite, or perhaps because of, its historical complexity, the church is a place of great beauty and character.

Some of this comes from exquisite details, such as the human head and

foliage on the capital supporting the eastern arch in the aisle, or the even finer work on the continuous arcading above the clerestory windows. Here you can also see evidence for the development of the building in the medieval period, for the eastern three clerestory windows on both sides are plain. Evidently the medieval masons had a short break here before changing to the much more elaborate design of the remaining windows. A similar change can be seen in the lower windows of the south wall, where the eastern one has a different head from the other three.

The church contains several exceptional works of art, especially in the north aisle, which bear testimony to the patronage by George Howard, ninth Earl of Carlisle, of the Arts and Crafts movement. Three windows here were designed by Edward Burne-Jones and made by William Morris's company. The left-hand window in the north wall is the earliest (1877), while the one in the west wall of the north aisle was inserted in 1890. The most easterly of the three is a much later example

Right: This window in the west wall of the north aisle, one of the three stained glass windows here by Morris & Co., depicts the Annunciation of Jesus' birth to the Shepherds

(1912) of Morris & Company's work carried out after the deaths of both Morris and Burne-Jones, and is inferior to the other two in execution (though the design seems to be the artist's original work). Burne-Jones also collaborated with Sir Edgar Boehm and Philip Webb on the memorial to Charles Howard (George's father), above the choir stalls on the left-hand side of the chancel. A further stained glass window was installed in the north aisle to commemorate Lady Cecilia Maude Roberts, née Howard (who put Lanercost into state guardianship in 1929), after her death in 1947. It depicts St Cecilia, set in scenery inspired by the Lanercost area, and was designed by the Irish

❖ THE LANERCOST CROSS ❖

The church interior has one exceptional medieval feature, though one that was never intended to rest here. The blocked doorway at the west end of the aisle now houses the shaft of the Lanercost Cross. The decoration down its sides marks out a central panel containing an inscription dated to the year 1214. This has suffered much damage in subsequent centuries and is now incomplete, but the full text was recorded by Lord William Howard in 1607. The cross originally stood outside the church, a short distance to the north of the west front. Its base can still be seen there, with the stump still in place. The cross has been in its current position since 1888.

The central section of the Lanercost Cross. Part of the inscription was hacked off so that the burial of two-year-old Robert could be recorded on 20 July 1657 (top). The full inscription (in Latin) was: 'In the 1214th year from the Incarnation, and the seventh year of the Interdict, Innocent III holding the apostolic see, Otto being emperor in Germany, Philip reigning in France, John in England, William in Scotland, this cross was made'

artist Evie Hone. Other windows and memorials commemorate several of Lanercost's eighteenth- and nineteenth-century clergy.

Lanercost's pews are also interesting. Two of them have medieval ends with 'poppyhead' carving, and one also has a human figure (a canon?), in a curious posture, perhaps at prayer. The remaining pews are Victorian, taking these medieval bench-ends as the inspiration for their shape.

THE PRECINCT

Leave the nave to re-enter the outer parts of the monastic precinct. The cross base is immediately to your right, while the vicarage and Vicar's

Pele are to your left. Abbey Farm lies beyond them, on the far left-hand side of the precinct. The outer gatehouse is in front of you, with the precinct wall running along the right side of the field.

Vicarage and Vicar's Pele

The vicarage continues to serve as the residence of Lanercost's parish clergy, and the house is not open to the public. Its main features can be appreciated from the outside.

The vicarage probably has medieval origins – especially the tower at its east end known as the Vicar's Pele – but it was incorporated into the post-Dissolution Dacre house. Many of its architectural features (windows, doors etc) belong to this period, though some blocked openings in the pele may be medieval. The battlements and largely blank walls of the tower present an aura of strength and defence that was clearly appropriate for the unsettled political world of the borders. The vicarage under-went significant renovations during the nineteenth century, and good-quality interiors of this date (and

Left: This remarkable photograph, which pre-dates the second phase of Victorian restoration of the church, shows thirteen pairs of pews. A drawing in 1849 by Antony Salvin, who was responsible for the first phase of the restoration, shows only eight pairs, though this may have been dictated by the perspective of his view (see page 30)

The south side of the Vicar's Pele in a drawing of c.1830

Many local families can trace generations of ancestors in the churchyard, not least the Earls of Carlisle. Members of the Howard family continue to be buried at Lanercost, though in the graveyard rather than the east end of the priory church

earlier) survive. The long frontage with the two-storey porch near its east end leads the eye pleasingly towards the west front of the church.

Churchyard

The north-eastern quarter of the precinct has been in use as the parish burial ground at least since the seventeenth century (when its registers begin), and it may have been in use since the medieval period. A medieval burial was uncovered just to the west of the vicarage in the late nineteenth century, but there could have been separate burial areas for canons and parishioners. One of the tombs is that of local resident Thomas Addison (1793–1860), a distinguished physician of Guy's Hospital who discovered the disease which was named after him. Look carefully at the gravestones and you will see some good eighteenth-century examples with symbolic decoration (such as skulls, crossed bones and hour-glasses) typical of its day.

Abbey Farm

Abbey Farm is owned by the Howard family and currently is not open to the public. Its main buildings can be viewed from the precinct.

Abbey Farm was probably designed by Antony Salvin in 1859, although parts of the farm buildings are certainly of earlier origin. It is built around two courtyards, with a farmhouse to the south-east. The northern range that passes across both courtyards has several seventeenth- and eighteenth-century datestones, and only required conversion or rebuilding in the nineteenth century. Salvin's new structures make a fine group, but the most important building here is the barn to the east of the courtyards.

This is of much earlier origin, with several blocked windows in its east wall showing that it was definitely in use during the Dacre residency from the sixteenth to the early eighteenth century. The barn may be of monastic origin.

Outer Gatehouse and Precinct Wall

The outer gatehouse formed the portal between the outside world and the closed world of the canons. The surviving part would have been the arch of the gatehouse facing into the precinct, and the building would have extended to the edge of the main road. The current gates were erected during George Howard's restorations, and reflect his Arts and Crafts interests.

The gatehouse arch was linked to the precinct wall. The western section of the wall no longer survives, but a low bank running north and south marks its position and probably covers its foundations. The entire northern stretch of the wall survives

Left: The surviving inner arch of the priory gatehouse, viewed from the west

Below: The intact gatehouse at nearby Wetheral Priory (now in the care of English Heritage) gives a good idea of what Lanercost's entrance would have looked like

in good condition. The grassy area between the outer gatehouse and the west front of the church may be where Edward I's 'temporary palace' was built (see page 22), although geophysical survey here has not identified any obvious buildings – possibly because most of them were temporary timber structures.

Below: This 1805 drawing of Lanercost by Joseph Powell shows the steep and wooded north side of the Irthing valley behind the priory, and the bridge over the river in the foreground. Note the second bridge (demolished later in the nineteenth century) on the left-hand side of the drawing. Buildings of the Dacre residence and the Abbey Farm can be seen behind the second bridge – these all pre-date the wholesale reconstruction of the farm and demolition of parts of the Dacre house in the mid-nineteenth century

HISTORY OF THE PRIORY

❖

Right: The coat of arms of the de Vaux family, in a marginal illustration from the Lanercost Cartulary. The cartulary is a rich source of information about the priory. It contains copies of various charters and other legal documents describing and defining its estates. The many illustrations in the margins are fascinating in their own right, giving a glimpse of medieval life in the monastic community

FOUNDATION

Lanercost Priory sits within the once hotly contested borderlands between England and Scotland. Even after the Normans captured Carlisle in 1092, much of the land to the east stayed within the Scottish realm. This included the area known as Gilsland, with Lanercost at its heart. The English did not finally gain control here until 1157, when King Henry II wrested control of the north from the Scots.

To consolidate his control over Gilsland, Henry chose a tactic that had worked well elsewhere in the north – he established a new overlord at Gilsland, Hubert de Vaux, and encouraged the foundation of a monastery by the second generation of the new ruling family. Hubert died in 1164, and his son Robert founded the Augustinian priory at Lanercost in his memory. The exact date at which he did this is not clear, but

1169 was the year traditionally accepted within the monastic community. Robert de Vaux was trying to secure his family's future in the afterlife: his priory was founded so that prayers could be said for ever (or so he thought) on behalf of his family. He also showed his loyalty to Henry II by asking for prayers to be said on his behalf as well.

The priory lay in secluded ground where the ancient Carlisle to Newcastle road follows the valley of the River Irthing. The river offered a good supply of water – an important factor in the planning of monasteries. The valley sides were heavily wooded, and this was another important natural resource. The first buildings would probably have been of timber because this allowed the community to become established more rapidly, though they would soon have set about constructing the stone buildings we see today. Timber would still have been needed for scaffolding, roofing and firewood.

Lanercost was also well positioned to exploit another local resource – Hadrian's Wall. The great Roman frontier provided a ready-made source of good building stone, cut to shape and easy to use. It was also the northern boundary of the priory's estates for about five miles. Not surprisingly, some of the walls are largely or wholly built of re-used Roman stone. Several stones bear traces of Roman inscriptions or carvings (see box, page 9).

THE AUGUSTINIANS

Renewal and reform had been a strong feature of Christianity in Europe during the tenth and eleventh centuries, largely because the religious way of life had deteriorated dramatically in the previous century.

The very concept of Christian monastic life had been shaken by accusations of corruption. Church reformers therefore went back to basics, using the rules laid down for religious communities by St Benedict and others. Some advocated a simple, very austere way of life as the best means of approaching the central tasks of worship and observance (for example the Cistercians and the Carthusians), but the Augustinians adopted a different approach. They originated in Italy and southern France in 1059, and believed that clergy serving in cathedrals and churches should live communally according to monastic principles. Augustinians were therefore canons (literally, priests serving in a cathedral) rather than monks, and used the Rule of St Augustine of Hippo – a less harsh and more flexible code.

Curiously this sometimes led to dissatisfaction among Lanercost's canons, some of whom wanted a more strict religious life. In 1282 Canon Hugh of Ireland returned to his homeland 'to enter stricter religion', while John of Newcastle had moved from Lanercost to the Cistercian community at Holmcultram in the previous year. Nevertheless the Augustinians were popular in the north-west, with important priories at Carlisle Cathedral, Cartmel and Hexham in England, and Jedburgh in Scotland.

St Augustine of Hippo, a fifth-century bishop whose writings formed the basis of the Augustinian rule of monastic life

THE ART ARCHIVE/ABBEY OF NOVACELLO OR NEUSTIFT/DAGLI ORTI

CUMBRIA RECORD OFFICE

Left: This drawing of an oak tree in a margin of the Lanercost Cartulary shows the importance of the woodlands owned by the priory

Medieval Patrons

By the time Lanercost was founded, many Anglo-Norman families had become established in the north-west despite intermittent conflict with Scotland. Hubert de Vaux was actually of southern stock, owning estates in Devon, and we know little of his short career in the north-west. His son founded Lanercost Priory, and most of its estate was donated by members of the de Vaux family, their successors to the lordship of Gilsland, or other families directly linked to them.

Major benefactors commonly expected to be buried in 'their' monasteries, at least from the thirteenth century onwards, partly in the hope that this would improve their chances of attaining salvation. Lanercost's benefactors were no exception. Robert de Vaux's son, also Robert, seems to have started the trend: he died between 1234 and 1237, leaving his body to the canons. His successor, another Hubert de Vaux, died soon afterwards (around 1240), and with him the de Vaux line at Lanercost died out. The barony of Gilsland – and with it the patronage of Lanercost – passed to Thomas de Multon. He had already married into the de Vaux line, and soon gave land to the priory to secure the right of burial

there. In about 1315 Randolf de Dacre married Margaret of Multon, and the Dacres' long dominance of Lanercost began. They also exercised the 'right' to be buried at Lanercost, often within the priory church rather than in the canons' cemetery outside it. Some of the medieval tomb slabs in the east end of the church, and others in storage, may have marked the last resting places of such men and women.

Life at the Priory

We know surprisingly little about the monastic community at Lanercost, although we do know the names of some priors (heads of the community), and that most of the canons were local men. Nor is it clear how many canons were in residence at any one time. The priory was certainly not especially large, and for much of its existence even the bare minimum of the prior and twelve canons seems to have been beyond its reach. This was a symbolically important number for the church, matching the numbers at the Last Supper. We know that in 1503 there were fewer than twelve canons here. Ironically our best evidence comes from the very people who would close the priory down at the Dissolution of the Monasteries. Their report on Lanercost in 1536 noted that Prior John Robinson led a community of eight canons and a

The wall-tomb and monument supposedly of Sir Roland Vaux in the north transept. However, Roland was alive in the thirteenth century, whereas the form and style of the tomb-monument suggest a date of 1350–1410. It is most likely to mark the grave of a member of the Dacre family

DAILY LIFE AT LANERCOST

❖   ❖

The routine of Augustinian religious life was similar to that of other orders. Much time was spent in private prayer and devotion, but the whole community – except those who were ill or infirm – gathered in the church seven times a day to celebrate offices (services), each at a specific time of day. In this as in other respects, however, the canons enjoyed an easy ride compared to other orders such as the Benedictines and Cistercians. Their offices were the shorter ones of the secular clergy – as priests, they had duties that other monks would not have.

Left: One of Lanercost's Augustinian canons depicted in the cartulary. Note the de Vaux arms above his head

Below: Lanercost Priory in a marginal illustration from the cartulary. The church is shown with a spire

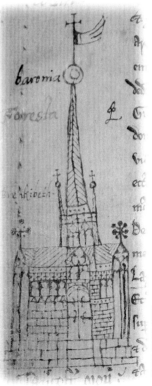

curate – ten in all. At least this was better than the community could achieve in 1379, when only the prior and four canons were accounted for.

The priory was given several churches at various times, such as Brampton, Farlam, Irthington and Walton. The canons might help at these, and many of them served directly as parish priests which took them beyond the confines of the priory, and also brought the whole income of the relevant church to the priory. Lanercost itself was the most important parish: in 1287 the priory church gained parochial status; by 1314 it had its own priest, and the nave of the priory became the parish church – a fact that saved it from destruction at the Dissolution.

Servants helped in the priory and out on the estates, augmenting the community's numbers. There were probably more servants than canons at most times. In 1536, for instance, the ten religious men were joined by around 40 servants, two of whom were women. Some helped to conduct services in church, while others looked after the catering, the buildings, and important agricultural tasks in field and barn. Agriculture was critical to the priory, for it had to be self-sufficient, or very nearly so. This was an important function of the 'colonising' monasteries of the eleventh and twelfth centuries in northern England. Much of the land given to Lanercost was of poor quality and previously unproductive.

Above: Marginal illustration in the Lanercost Cartulary showing Gamel of Walton, a servant of the priory, wielding a pitchfork

Below: A portrait of King Edward I from the Lanercost Cartulary. Comparison with other contemporary depictions of the king suggests that this is a reasonable likeness

It was in the canons' own interests to improve and exploit it, because the income from the lands and churches had to pay for everything – the building and upkeep of their church, their clothes, food and drink. As a result, they became major landlords in the area, and even if the servants did the bulk of the work the management of the estates must have been a distraction from the religious vocation. This distraction must have been minor, however, compared with the disruption caused after Edward I began his campaigns against the Scots.

EDWARD I AND LANERCOST

Lanercost Priory is unusual among English monasteries because it became a royal palace for more than five months in 1306–7 under Edward I. His visit was symptomatic of England's problems with Scotland, as from 1296 onwards the two countries were effectively at war. Immediately Lanercost was in the front line, for in April 1296 a Scottish army crossed the border leaving mayhem in its wake. They stayed overnight at the priory and burnt some buildings (probably timber ones in the outer precinct) as they went. This was to be a grim portent of things to come, for raids would feature regularly over the coming decades.

Scottish kings regularly imposed themselves upon their country's monasteries, and royal palaces grew up at Dunfermline and Holyrood abbeys. English monarchs usually restrained themselves to a few nights as monastic guests when their journeys required it. Edward I's time at Lanercost was different. He had already visited the priory briefly in 1280 and 1300, making gifts on both occasions. In 1306, however, he was an old man of 67 on campaign, and his health was poor. The route north had been slow, and illness dogged him on the journey west along Hadrian's Wall to Carlisle. When Edward arrived at Lanercost on 28 September, carried on a litter, it was clear that he could go no further.

The king was accompanied by Queen Margaret, noblemen, bodyguards, servants, doctors and others – perhaps 200 people or more. A medieval royal progress was something to behold, with great wagon trains carrying food, equipment and furniture while the royal party itself went ahead on horseback. And now Lanercost Priory had to accommodate them all. Masons and carpenters erected separate suites of buildings for the king and queen, and more buildings and tents were put up for the accompanying masses. The queen's suite included a bathhouse, and several fireplaces were provided at considerable expense for warmth in the northern winter. All the buildings had to be within the precinct walls for security. Although the king rarely favoured the church with his presence – both his suite and the queen's contained private chapels – the cloister was a convenient and pleasant place for walking. On 14 February 1307 Edward paid 16*s* 3*d* for making gutters there, presumably to remove rainwater more efficiently.

Edward's stay disrupted every aspect of monastic life. However, the king could not continue his journey during the harsh northern winter, and he was not well enough to move on to Carlisle until March 1307. He had given very little money to the priory: the community complained that it had been 'greatly impoverished and brought low' by the cost of his stay and the strain it had put on their lives. They hoped for much and got little, other than the gift of churches at Carlatton and Mitford (Northumberland), which offered the prospect of long-term income from their rents.

This reconstruction painting shows the priory after parts of the cloister had been rebuilt in the thirteenth century. Note the new chapter house on the east (right) side of the cloister. (Reconstruction by Peter Dunn)

DEBTS AND DECLINE

Both Lanercost's church and its estates were targets during Scottish raids. Any decrease in the priory's revenue from its estates could leave it on a knife-edge. A survey in 1302 showed that its property at Farlam had been utterly destroyed, while the values of Brampton, Walton and Irthington had been reduced by one-third. It was not as though this was a one-off problem, to be resolved by rapid rebuilding. Edward I died later in 1307 near Burgh by Sands, Cumberland, after he had left the priory, and his son Edward II was so beset by political problems at court that he gave little attention to the north. The king of Scotland needed no further encouragement, and large-scale raids were resumed with a vengeance. Lanercost was once more in the direct line of fire, and in 1311 the Scottish king himself, Robert Bruce, led an army to the priory's door. The damage he did in three days came at a time when the priory's resources were still depleted after Edward I's stay. The buildings themselves did not suffer too badly, but the priory's other properties suffered wholesale destruction. In 1346 a large Scottish army crossed the border and plundered the church, which must have been another severe blow to the morale and life of the priory.

The Scots were not the only concern at this time, for famine was prevalent in 1316 and cattle were hit by disease three years later. The Black Death of 1349 is unlikely to have left the community entirely unscathed. The canons must have felt beset by problems on all sides, but they scarcely helped themselves when internal dissension broke out in the mid-fourteenth century. This came to a head in 1355 when the election of a new prior split the community. Some chose John de Novyngton while others supported Richard de Ridale. Bishop Welton of Carlisle came down in Ridale's favour, and backed up his choice by visiting Lanercost again in 1356; however, Richard gave up his post in November 1360. Open warfare with Scotland restarted in 1384, and in December 1386 Lanercost's prior was captured and held to ransom by the Scots. In April 1409 Henry Bowet, Archbishop of York, recognised the utter depths to which the priory had sunk through these various troubles and urged everyone in his province to help the poor canons.

Over the next 100 years the priory's fortunes became more stable, and gradually improved. Mostly this was achieved through careful economic management. Cutbacks were made where necessary, and the canons pursued debts even more vigorously than before. They also sold off more distant properties, concentrating on the core estates. In spite of these efforts the community remained poor. Its value in 1536 was assessed at a little over £85, and even if this was an underestimate it was still a dramatic decline from around 1300 when the income had been more than £200.

The seal of Robert Bruce, king of Scotland 1306–29, showing him on horseback

THE DISSOLUTION OF THE MONASTERIES

The figure of £200 was that set by Henry VIII in the 1530s as the upper limit for the closure of the lesser monasteries. Any monastic community worth less than this could expect closure after an Act of Parliament had been passed in 1536.

Lanercost's canons' worst fears were realised when Sir Thomas Wharton arrived on 16 July 1536 to survey their estates. The uprising known as the Pilgrimage of Grace won them a reprieve, though Lanercost apparently took no part in the revolt. On 4 March 1537 the Duke of Norfolk, acting on the king's behalf, ordered the closure of the priory.

Strangely, Norfolk then decided to put the priory into temporary custody – and chose the prior and 'certain religious [men] of the graver sort' as his custodians! But this was only a temporary reprieve, and no doubt the progress of demolition

Lanercost Priory in the aftermath of Henry VIII's Dissolution of the Monasteries – compare with the reconstruction on page 23. The refectory has been removed, and the east cloister range completely demolished. (Reconstruction by Peter Dunn)

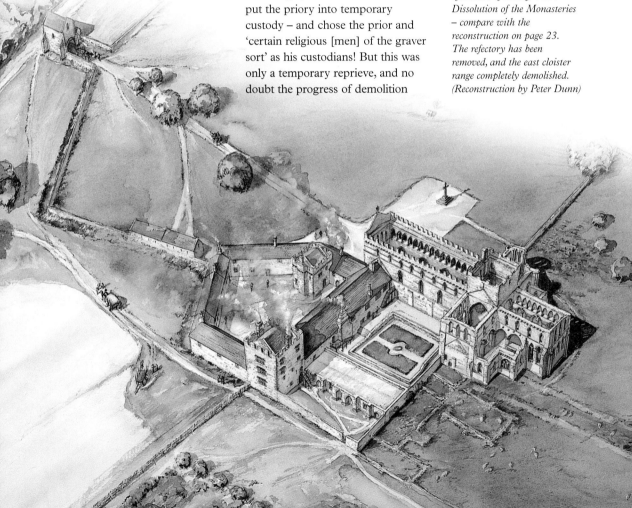

The funeral banner of Thomas, 2nd Baron Dacre of Gilsland (1467-1525), which is now in the College of Arms

works on their cloister, and especially the refectory (dining room), brought this home to the canons. Finally, on 8 January 1538, Lanercost Priory was closed and what was left of its community was dispersed. John Robinson, the last prior, had already been granted a pension of £8 per year. Most of the other canons received one-off payments of 40s (£2), though two received nothing: they already had incomes from Brampton and Irthington where they were the vicars. The curate at Lanercost, John Blacklock, was effectively sacked, and given 33s 4d (£1.66). Christopher Snawden, who had also been a canon at the priory, took over the curacy. Finally the servants were paid off, with amounts ranging from 20d (8p) to 20s (£1).

Lanercost still needed its parish church. The nave of the priory church had been used as such for more than 200 years, and it made sense for this to continue. The east end of the church was kept up for a few years because of the chantry – an arrangement whereby prayers would be said for a dead person's soul, in exchange for a donation of land or money. The chantry was set up by Mabel, Lady Dacre, in 1503 in memory of her husband, Humphrey,

Lord Dacre, the first Baron Dacre of Gilsland (d.1485), and continued until Humphrey's grandson, William, Lord Dacre (1500-63), withdrew his interest in it. William had hoped to take over at Lanercost in the wake of the Dissolution, but he was thwarted. There was another Dacre in the wings, and the crown had an interest in encouraging the rival.

Lanercost and the Dacres

William, 3rd Lord Dacre was out of favour with Henry VIII. His steadfast adherence to Catholicism was unlikely to attract royal approval, and he barely escaped conviction for treason in 1534. Despite this William was very much a power locally, having his seat at Naworth Castle, close to Lanercost. Unfortunately for him, he had a half-brother, Thomas Dacre (d.1565), an illegitimate son of Thomas, 2nd Lord Dacre. Thomas was a strong supporter of the royal cause, and already the deputy of Sir William Penyson, a colourful character who had been put in charge of Lanercost in 1538. Four years later the king granted the priory and its lands to Thomas, specifically excluding the parish church and its cemetery.

The door had been shut firmly in William's face, and Thomas consolidated his position in a number of ways. He fought at Solway Moss in 1542, and became a deputy warden of the marches in 1552. He also supported Protestantism enthusiastically. Even so the parishioners at Lanercost were to be responsible for maintaining the parish church (the nave of the former priory), while Thomas made arrangements for the east end of the church – the family vault of his half-brother – to become his own last resting place. The lords of Naworth moved their allegiance to the cathedral at Carlisle, and so a new Dacre line was in control at Lanercost.

The Protestant Dacres needed a house to live in, and it is to this that we owe part of Lanercost's preservation. Thomas decided that the west range of the monastic cloister would make a good residence. The first floor was converted into a great open hall – now known as Dacre Hall, and used as the village hall – with a grand new

fireplace in its east wall. The south end linked to the Dacre Tower, which was probably late medieval in origin but largely rebuilt, or converted, by the Dacres. A service range (now lost) ran west from the tower. The grounds were provided with a rabbit warren, a dovecote, a garden and an orchard. Thomas began all this, but the work was probably completed by his son Christopher (d.1593), whose initials and the date 1586 are carved into the fireplace.

For a while the Dacres of Lanercost prospered in their new residence. Their rivals at Naworth had troubles of their own, for the male line died out when the infant George, grandson of William, Lord Dacre, was killed when his vaulting horse collapsed under him in 1568. His three sisters became wards of Thomas Howard, 4th Duke of Norfolk,

The Dacres of Lanercost not only had a fashionable mansion after the Dissolution, but they also provided it with fine grounds, as shown in Samuel and Nathaniel Buck's engraving of the priory seen from the south in 1739. Note that the nave of the church is unroofed at this date

who married them to his three sons: the youngest sister, Elizabeth – whose inheritance included the Gilsland barony – married Lord William Howard. The duke was executed for his plan to marry Mary, Queen of Scots, and for a while the Howard and Dacre lands became crown properties; it was not until 1603 that Lord William Howard was restored to his Cumberland estates. Meanwhile the Lanercost Dacres began to fall into debt, and fought on the losing side in the civil wars of the mid-seventeenth century. The last male heir, James, died unmarried at the age of 30 on 16 July 1716 with debts of more than £1800. It was not a good end for the Dacres of Lanercost.

The parish church fared badly during this era. In 1597 the church was described as being in poor condition. With little money to support its upkeep, the once-great monastic nave began the steady decline that was to culminate in its abandonment towards the end of the seventeenth century, when the congregation retreated into the north aisle. This was given a neat slate roof, while the nave roof was either left to fall, or taken down. Some form of partition wall must have been built between the great piers separating the nave and the aisle.

THE 18TH AND 19TH CENTURIES

The extinction of the Lanercost Dacre line saw the priory estate and the right to appoint vicars to the parish briefly going in different directions. The Howard lords of Naworth became Earls of Carlisle after Lord William Howard's great-grandson was granted the title by Charles II in 1661 (it was

The Buck brothers' view of Lanercost Priory from the north in 1739 shows again the roofless nave, but most of the north aisle is roofed; this was still in use as the parish church. Note the porches in front of both north doors – these appear to have been demolished in the nineteenth century

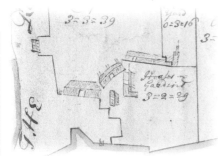

the third earl who began Castle Howard in 1699). Naworth itself was still very much in use, and the earl wanted to regain control of the priory. He succeeded when the crown leased him the site in 1718. The appointment of vicars, meanwhile, had passed to Joseph Appleby, James Dacre's cousin and heir. It was probably with his debts in mind that the Applebys sold Lanercost's right to appoint vicars to the earl in 1736, thus reuniting the secular and spiritual estates.

The parish had 296 families in 1747, twenty-one of whom were nonconformists. There were clearly too many people to fit into the north aisle. In the 1730s, therefore, the parish had sought permission to raise funds to extend back into the old nave by rerooofing it. This was granted in 1738, and work was completed by 1747. The new roof was of slate with a flat ceiling underneath it.

Lanercost also became a visitor attraction in the later eighteenth century. In 1774 William Hutchinson commented on the 'solemnity of the situation'. This feeling for the site's picturesque and romantic qualities was accompanied by the drier but equally valuable interest of antiquarians and archaeologists.

By the end of the eighteenth century the church fabric was threatened by the 'profusion of ivy, ash and other plantings' growing on the walls. The whole site drifted towards decay. The Earl of Carlisle was the one man in the area with enough money to do something about this, but his interests were diverted by the disastrous fire of 1844 which destroyed much of Naworth Castle. Fortunately he appointed the architect Antony Salvin to look after its rebuilding. Salvin's career was still in its early days, but he was forging a good reputation both for grand houses and churches. He was asked to look into the state of the church and ruins in 1846. His report made stark reading: £2000 worth of work was required, about half of it on the church.

The crown instructed Salvin to get on with work around the ruins, but a three-way argument broke out between the crown, the Earl of Carlisle and the

Left: This detail from an estate map of 1724 shows what was left of the priory. The west cloister range and Dacre Tower are clearly identifiable, while the building running diagonally to the west of the church appears to be the vicarage. (Howard of Naworth plan 202/1)

Below: Thomas Hearne recorded what he saw at Lanercost with an accurate eye while also acknowledging its visual power. His engraving of the crossing ruins in 1777 was accompanied by a blank verse on 'Life's morality'

Above: George Howard's watercolour of Naworth Castle, c.1890, shows that he was a very talented artist himself, as well as being a major patron of the arts

Right: Antony Salvin (1799–1881) became one of the most respected architects of his day. His work tended towards the Gothic, which suited him well for working at Lanercost. His 1849 drawing of the intended restoration of the parish church shows his sensitivity to the priory's medieval architecture

parish as to who was responsible for the church's maintenance. Matters were brought to a head on 14 September 1847, when the roof at the east end of the church collapsed during a vicious storm. Salvin submitted a new, higher estimate for the work. Eventually the crown's commissioners made grants totalling £2780 in 1847–8 so that the works could be carried out. The architect and builders soon got to work, and the church was reopened with great ceremony on 12 August 1849.

Unusually for his day, Salvin retained original stone-work and features wherever possible. He even left medieval wall plaster in place, a most unusual decision for the time. Salvin was active elsewhere around the priory and Naworth estate as well, carrying out alterations in the vicarage during 1850–51 and designing a new farm (surely Abbey Farm) in 1859, both for the seventh Earl of Carlisle.

The seventh Earl died in 1864, and in the same year his young nephew, George Howard, married Rosalind Stanley. The couple spent their honeymoon at Naworth, and took to life here immediately. The eighth Earl remained in a Sussex nursing home due to his disabilities, but trustees had been running the estate since 1854; in his absence, George and Rosalind made several extended stays at Naworth. In 1868 the trustees offered to buy the Lanercost estate from the crown, probably at George's instigation, and despite the recent and heavy state expenditure there the sale

was agreed in 1869. Queen Victoria herself had insisted that the new owners should be legally bound to preserve the priory, ruins and all, but George needed no such prompting. He was a man of great talent and sensitivity, and Lanercost enjoyed its best years since the Dissolution under him. In 1889 he became the ninth Earl of Carlisle.

ARTS AND CRAFTS AT LANERCOST

George Howard ordered a second restoration during the 1870s under the local architect C. J. Ferguson. Where Salvin had largely been content to leave the interior as he had found it, Ferguson stripped plaster from the walls and re-ordered the furniture, probably altering pews that Salvin had originally put in. A new organ and choir stalls were installed, thus helping to define a distinct area for the chancel. A barrel vault was inserted inside Salvin's open timber roof. Ferguson also stopped up an entrance into the precinct next to the farm buildings, bringing visitors to the priory in through the historically correct route via the outer gatehouse.

George was a fine amateur artist, and a friend of leading figures in the Pre-Raphaelite and Arts and Crafts movements. He had the architect Philip Webb design an unusual new church at nearby Brampton, with magnificent stained glass windows by Edward Burne-Jones and William Morris's company. At Lanercost the same combination designed and installed three further windows at the north-west corner of the church.

LATER HISTORY

George Howard died in 1911 and was buried at Lanercost in the 'Lady Chapel' at the angle of the north transept and chancel, where his tombstone can still be seen. The priory passed to his daughter, Lady Cecilia Roberts, who could not afford the upkeep of the ruins. Fortunately the Ancient Monuments Consolidation and Amendment Act of 1913 enabled the Office of Works to take monuments of national importance into state guardianship, and Cecilia offered Lanercost as a candidate. On 1 January 1929 the ruins were handed over as a 'gift to the nation'.

HOWARDS OF NAWORTH

Above: Self-portrait of George Howard, c.1883

Below: Robert Carlyle's drawing of the priory gatehouse in 1792, showing a simple gate between short walls. Early photographs confirm that this arrangement survived into the late nineteenth century, probably being altered to the current state by C. J. Ferguson

TULLIE HOUSE MUSEUM

Below: Thomas Hearne's drawing of 1777 shows the east end of the priory church, the west cloister range and the Dacre Tower, with extensive vegetation on and around the ruins. The vegetation was finally cleared when the Ministry of Works took the ruins into guardianship in 1929

The Office of Works subsequently carried out substantial repairs to the priory buildings in the 1930s; they also undertook excavations in 1937 to reveal the east side of the cloister and its successive chapter houses.

Meanwhile maintenance of the church has been managed by the

parishioners, with appeals to fund major works. This has included arresting movement in the roof and south wall of the nave in 1976. In 1985 the roof was re-slated and all its timbers treated. The long tradition of artistic commissions in the church has continued through to the present, and an elegant glass plaque was erected on the north aisle wall in 2001 to commemorate the end of the second millennium.

As well as remaining a place of Christian worship, Lanercost today is a very active place: a busy programme of music, festivals, crafts, open-air theatre, and school and family events links the church, Dacre Hall and priory ruins as the hub of a thriving community.

HOWARDS OF NAWORTH

FURTHER READING

Allibone, G., *Antony Salvin: Pioneer of Gothic Revival Architecture, 1799–1881*, University of Missouri Press (1987). An excellent introduction to the architect with a catalogue of his work, including buildings at Lanercost.

Mawson, D. J. W., *Lanercost Landmarks, Wall Walkers and Watering Holes* (2001). A useful short guide to various aspects of local history.

Maxwell, H. (ed. and trans.), *The Chronicle of Lanercost, 1272–1346*, 2 vols., Llanerch Press (2001). Fascimile reprint of the 1913 edition.

Moorman, J. R. H., *Lanercost Priory* (1946; 2nd edn 1976). Guidebook to the parish church.

Robinson, D., *The Geography of Augustinian Settlement*, British Archaeological Reports (British Series), 80 (1980). A general description of the Augustinian order.

Summerson, H. and Harrison, S., *Lanercost Priory, Cumbria: A Survey and Documentary History*, Cumberland and Westmorland Antiquarian and Archaeological Society Research Series, 10 (2000). Full, very detailed description of the priory's history and buildings.

Todd, J. M. (ed.), *The Lanercost Cartulary*, Cumberland and Westmorland Antiquarian and Archaeological Society Record Series, 11 (1997). Modern transcribed edition of the cartulary, with reproductions of many marginal illustrations.

ACKNOWLEDGEMENTS

The author wishes to thank Malcolm Cooper, Henry Owen-John and David Sherlock of English Heritage, the Revd Canon Christopher Morris, John Lee, Mary Windle, David Willey, Marian Robinson, David Mawson, the Hon. Philip Howard, Roderick Ogilvy and Henry Summerson for reading and commenting on drafts of the guidebook text. Particular thanks are due to the editor, Katy Carter, for steering the guidebook through to publication so efficiently.